ME, MY DOG, AND A SHEEP

MELISSA MULLAMPHY

ILLUSTRATIONS BY
ANDREW THOMAS

© 2020 Melissa Mullamphy
All Rights Reserved.

No part of this publication may be reproduced, stored in a retrieval system, or transmitted, in any form or by any means, electronic, mechanical, photocopying, recording, or otherwise, without the written permission of the author.

ISBN (Paperback): 978-1-7348026-1-0
ISBN (Hardcover): 978-1-7348026-0-3

Printed in the United States of America

This is truly an underdog story of love, extraordinary people, and a dog with a huge heart who **NEVER GAVE UP.**

My name is Luke, and I want to tell you about a very special dog.

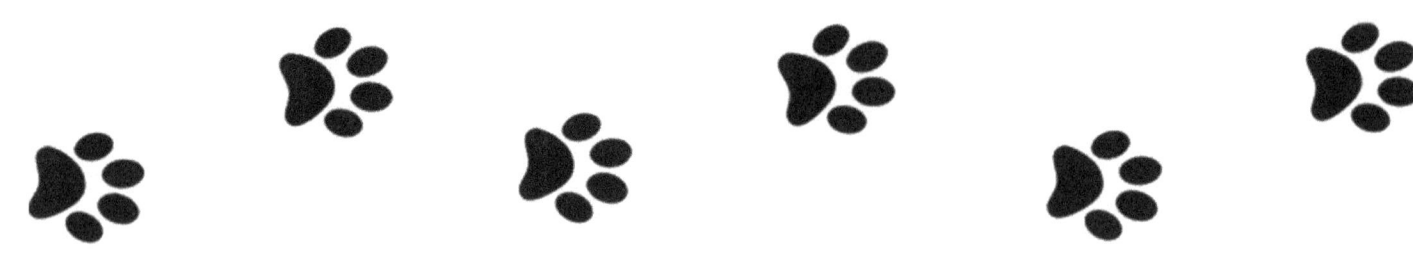

A big puppy lived in a small cage in a pet store. This dog was older and larger than most of the other puppies. At four-months-old, nobody wanted such a big pup. Then, one day my Daddy entered the store and spotted the hefty hound in the small pen and asked, "SIR, HOW MUCH IS THIS DOG?"

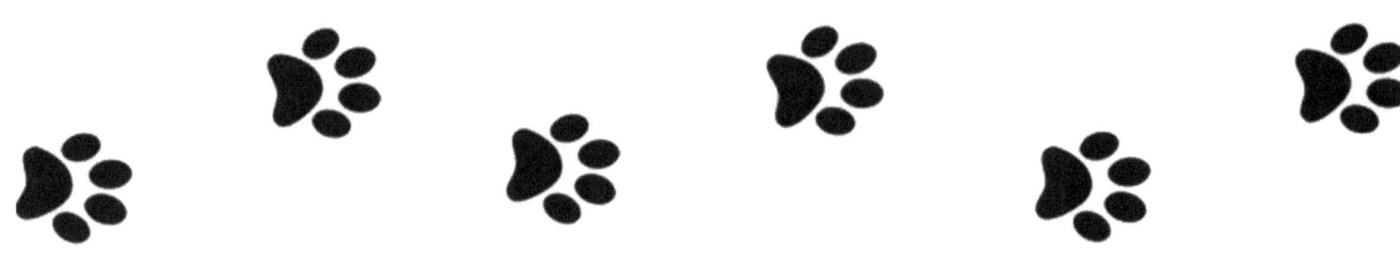

"Oh, that one? Nobody wants that one," replied the store owner.

"I do," my Dad said. And this is when the story of my dog, Grizzy, begins.

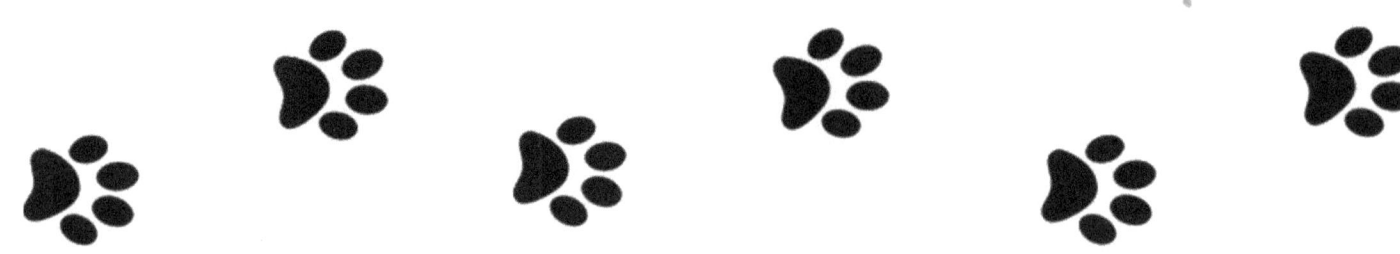

My Daddy gave me the puppy when I was two-years-old. I named him Grizzy, and he was my best friend. We did everything together. We slept together, played catch together, watched cartoons together—you name it!

Each morning after I woke up, I carried my blanket into the living room, and Grizzy snatched it from me. It was his way of saying "good morning." He never chewed it; he just pranced around with it to show me that he wanted to love the blanket, too.

For three years, Grizzy was my constant companion, until it was time for me to go to kindergarten. Each morning, Grizzy waited at the end of the driveway with me behind the fence, watching for the yellow bus that I rode to school. Grizzy barked and chased the bus as far as the fence would allow. When I returned from school, Grizzy was always there—wagging his tail and excited for me to get home so that we could run and play.

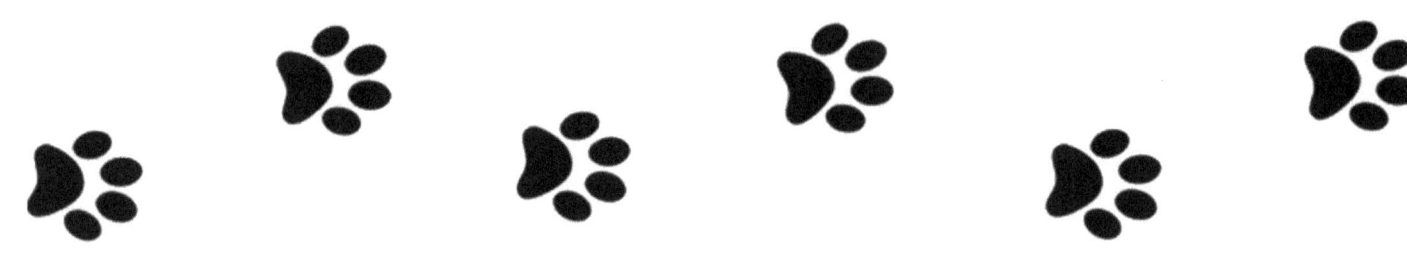

One day, Grizzy had a hard time getting up. My mom and I took Grizzy to an animal doctor, that said that Grizzy had injured his neck and needed surgery right away. We agreed to the operation. We did not have a choice because it had to be done for Grizzy to get better.

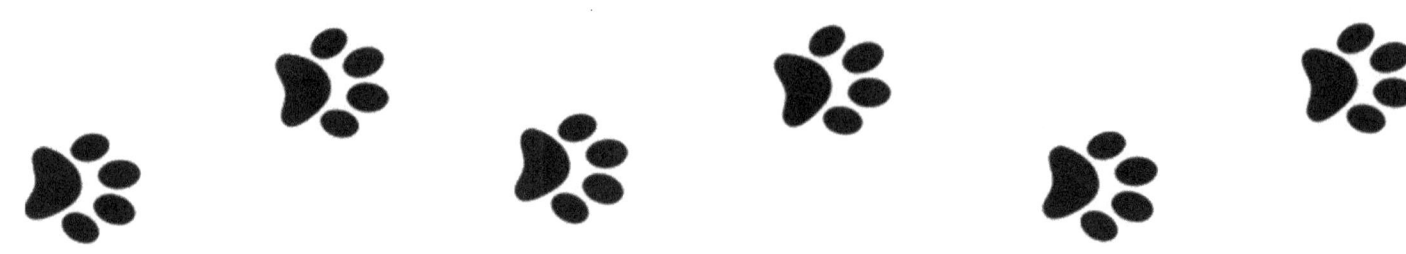

We brought Grizzy to the animal hospital for the procedure. The good news was that Grizzy walked into the animal hospital on his own four paws, but the bad news was that Grizzy could not walk out.

He was completely paralyzed.

It was April, and spring had arrived. All I wanted to do was race around outside with Grizzy. For months, Mommy, Daddy, and I tried everything to get poor Grizzy to move. We tried to exercise him and reward him with cookies, and we had special animal doctors come to the house. One day we even purchased Grizzy a wheelchair for dogs, but he did not have the strength to use it.

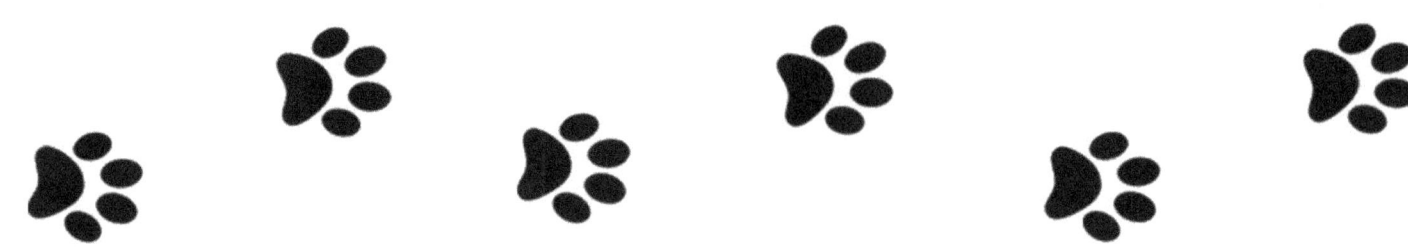

After four months, Grizzy's health had not improved. Our sad Grizzy could barely hold his head up without a pillow. In July, Mommy and Daddy found a special animal hospital that was far from our house. They said that this clinic offered Grizzy's last chance for recovery. When we left him with the animal doctors, we did not hold much hope; they said that he may never walk again. Our Grizzy had so much nerve damage that he had to learn how to walk, stand, sit, and hold his head up, poor Grizzy had to learn everything again!

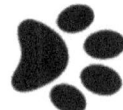

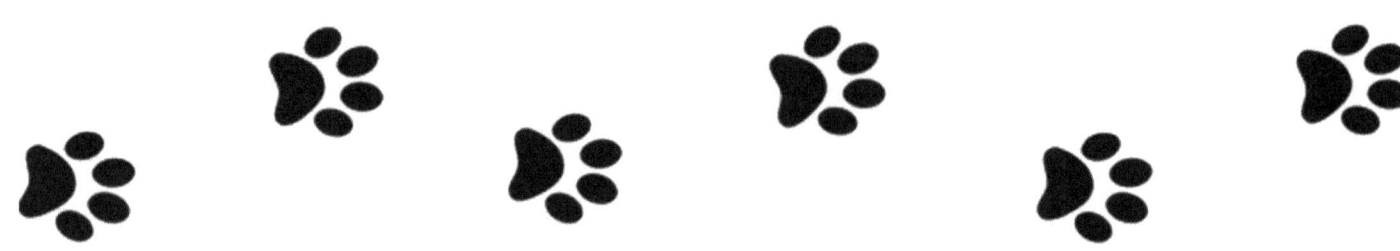

My mom said that it would take a leap of faith to leave Grizzy at the clinic until he regained his ability to walk, and that this undertaking would be very difficult for the staff and Grizzy.

When we left Grizzy at the hospital, we all cried, including Grizzy. It was a horrible moment.

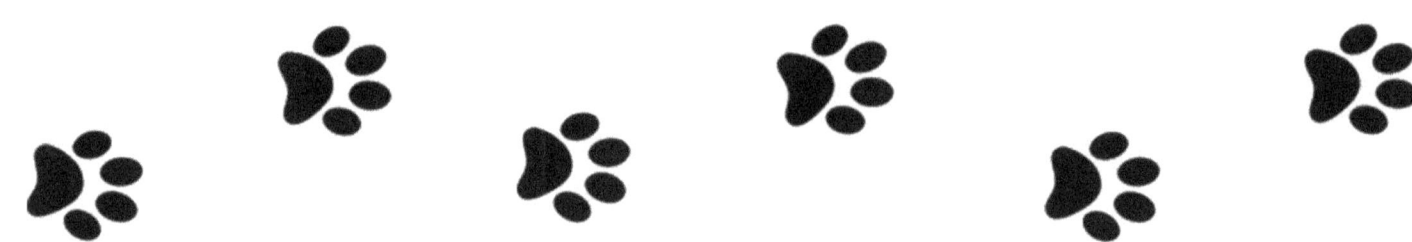

I want to tell you the names of the dog lovers who helped Grizzy because they are my friends now, too; they are Dr. Crowe, Jenn, Kellie, and Ken. Everyone at the clinic helped Grizzy.

For six months they worked with Grizzy—day and night. They loved Grizzy and tried everything possible to improve his condition. The goal was for Grizzy to walk.

One day Grizzy would move a toe, on another day he might wag his tail. Sometimes he attempted to roll on his side or even clean himself. Each step took a huge effort from Grizzy.

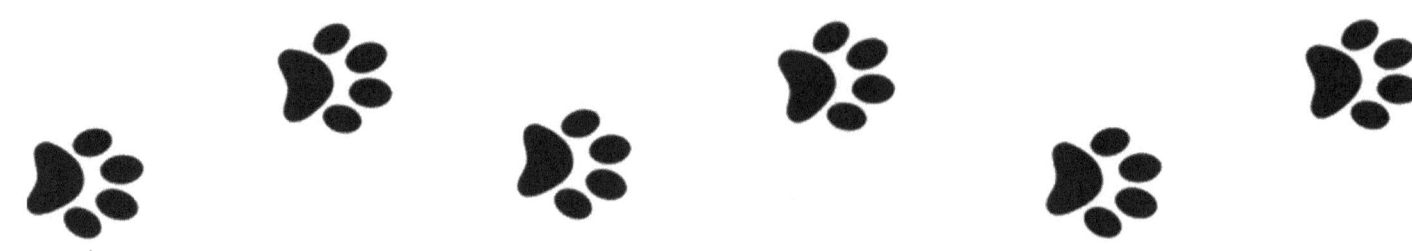

Because Grizzy had not walked in months, Dr. Crowe said that the muscles in his legs had wasted away; she recommended a water treadmill to strengthen them. Wobbler's Disease—that's the name of Grizzy's illness; it's a funny name, but it's not a funny illness. In fact, Dr. Crowe said that sometimes dogs don't get better when they have it.

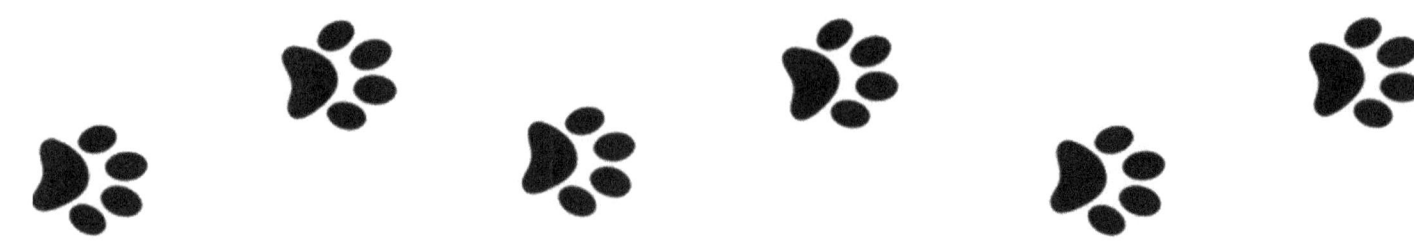

Mommy and I sometimes visited Grizzy on the weekends. Each visit brought happiness and sadness, especially when it was time to go home. I missed Grizzy so much!

By now you may be wondering, who is the sheep in the title of my story? "Sheepie" was a toy that Kellie and Jenn used. My mom said that Sheepie motivated and inspired Grizzy to move and exercise so that he could heal. Sheepie was a reward—kind of like a cookie—but it was a squeaky toy. The animal hospital workers were not the only ones to use Sheepie. They told us that Grizzy squeezed Sheepie to communicate.

Because Grizzy could not move, he alerted them with a squeak from Sheepie when he needed something, like a drink or a scratch on the head. The staff said that the toy was so important to Grizzy's therapy that he eventually collected six Sheepies!

In November, the clinic staff told us that Grizzy was displaying slow movements in attempts to stand. This was great news!

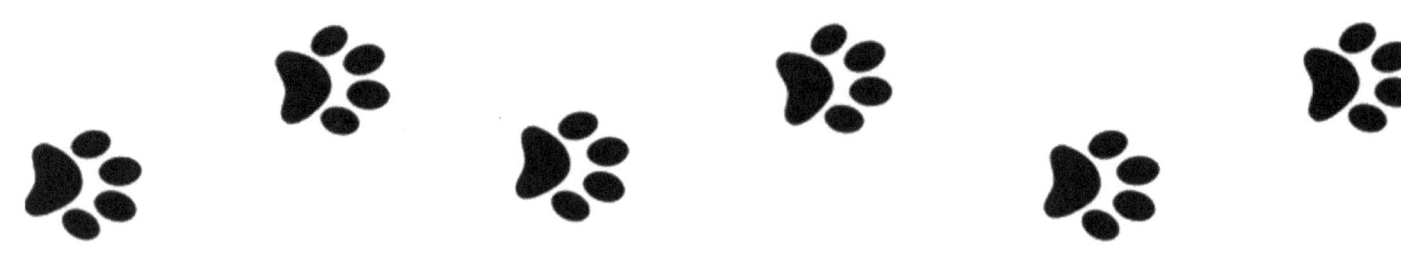

My mom said that Jenn and Kellie worked for hours to help him carry his weight and carefully place his feet and that their attention paid off. Although weak and still in need of support, two days before Christmas, **GRIZZY WALKED!**

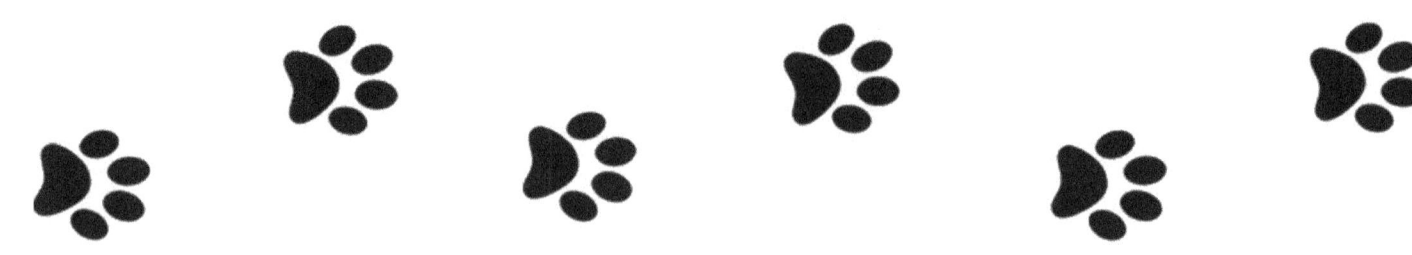

We were excited! Mom said that Grizzy defied the odds. He overcame his disability. And in January, we picked up Grizzy—our walking dog. (When he spotted us, he raced to the car.)

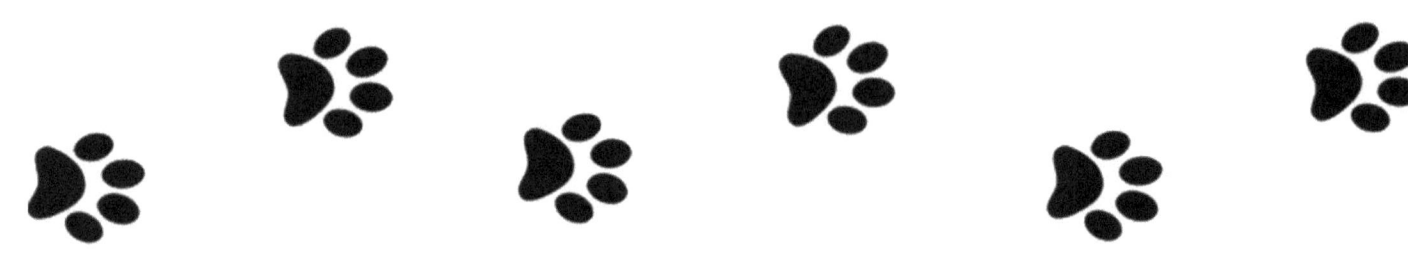

My parents and I think that if Grizzy could talk, he would encourage you to NEVER GIVE UP! THERE IS ALWAYS A CHANCE. IGNORE ANYONE WHO TELLS YOU THAT YOU CANNOT DO IT. ALWAYS TRY YOUR BEST. STAY POSITIVE. MIRACLES CAN HAPPEN!

Grizzy should know. **GRIZZY IS A MIRACLE.**

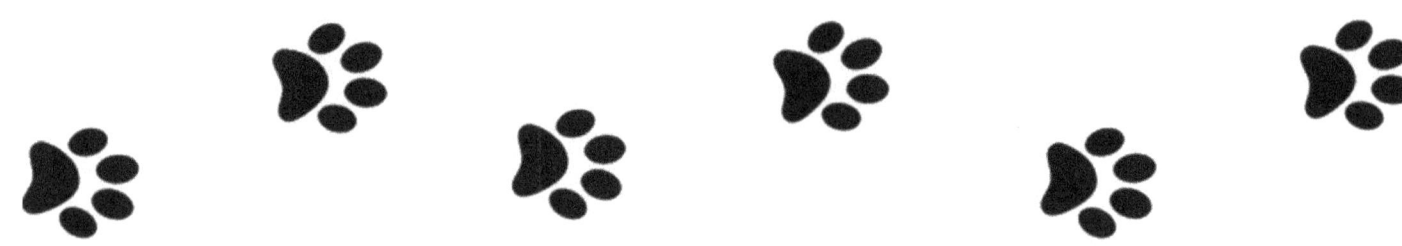

The animal hospital where Grizzy learned to walk again is a great place. Due to their care of Grizzy, I got my best buddy back. My parents are thankful for Grizzy's return, too. Today, I can shout that Mommy, Daddy, Grizzy, Sheepie, our other fur babies and I will live happily ever after.

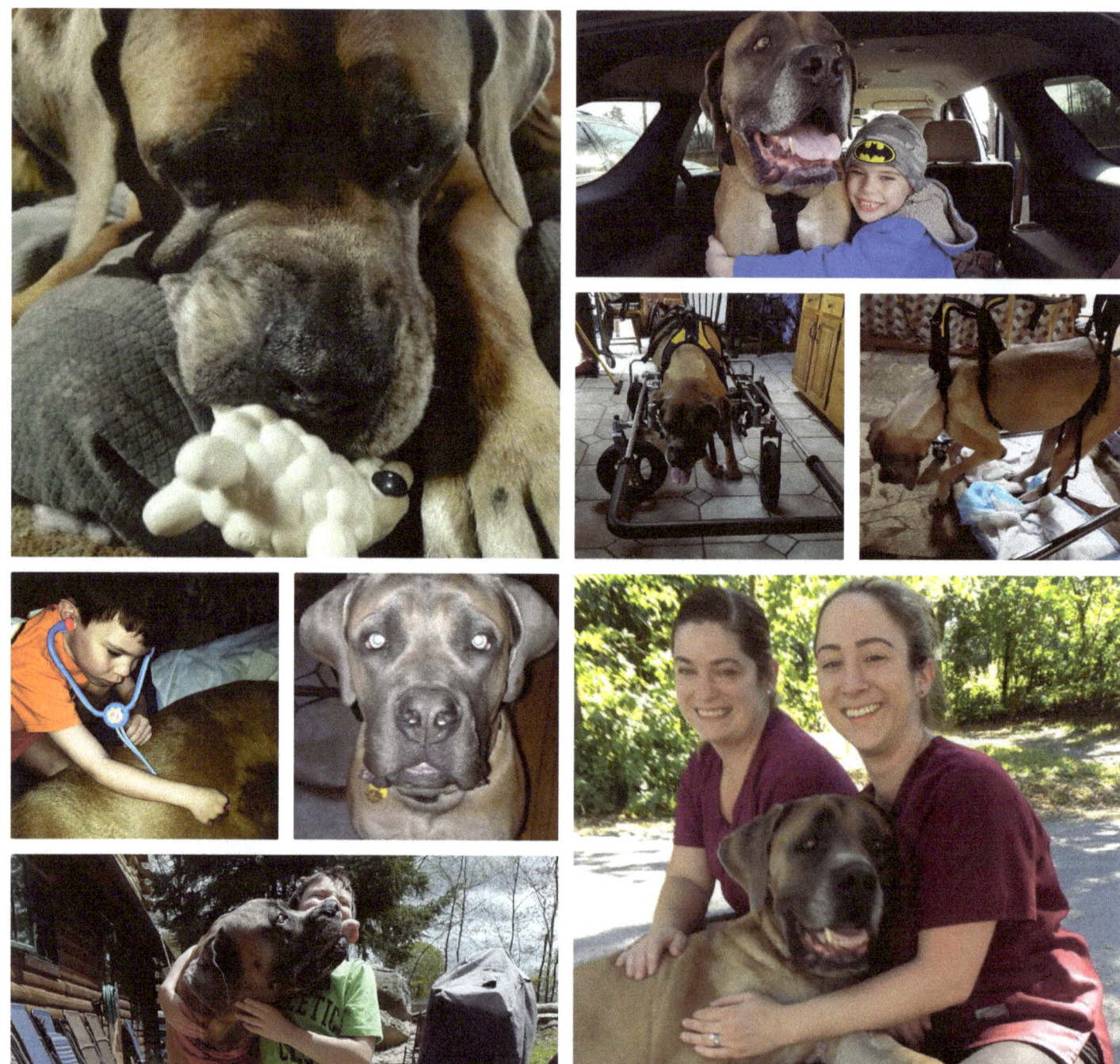

ACKNOWLEDGEMENTS

A special Thank You to the following: Shaker Animal Hospital, Albany, New York; Sarah Crowe, DVM, Certified Animal Acupuncturist and Chiropractor; Jenn Wolfe, LVT, CCRP; Kellie Lembo Strock, Rehab Team; Ken Wolfe, Hospital Manager; Patter Paws Animal Hospital, Pawling, New York; Christopher Proto, DVM; Whitney Will, DVM, Certified Animal Acupuncturist and Holistic Medicine Specialist; Sue Silva, with her editorial help in a pinch; Help 'Em Up™ Harness, the only way we could have achieved moving Grizzy around; and my *amazing* family. Their support during Grizzy's recovery bolstered me during very difficult times.

Your mental strength, drive, and attitude are as important, if not more, than your physical effort when you face a challenge. You cannot choose what happens to you, but you can choose how you handle it.

In this story, a close family deals with a dilemma with love, the support of caring professionals, and a big-hearted dog who did **NOT GIVE UP.** This book is dedicated to my son, Luke, who learned how to be selfless, compassionate, helpful, and strong at the age of six—with a can-do attitude and a special love for his dog, Grizzy.

ABOUT THE AUTHOR

Melissa Mullamphy was born in Westchester County, New York. She earned a Master's Degree in Counseling and Psychology from Marist College. For over twenty years, Melissa worked in the reinsurance industry and was employed by various hospitals and involved with many charities. Melissa married Anthony, her high-school sweetheart, while he was serving in the U.S. Marine Corps. Their life together has always included animals. They spoil them all and consider their pets family. In 2009, Melissa and Anthony were blessed with a miracle baby boy, Luke. This year, they celebrate their twenty-fifth wedding anniversary. Melissa, now retired, enjoys raising their wonderful little boy—the light of her eyes—and caring for their animal family, including, as you learned in this story, a special dog that did not give up.

www.ingramcontent.com/pod-product-compliance
Lightning Source LLC
Chambersburg PA
CBHW040044100526
44584CB00033BA/4264